Advance Praise for

My Heart is a Pomegranate/
Mi Corazón es una Granada

Jessica Helen Lopez wrangles poetry with a lasso of words that cut and bind to the heart! These poems, like pomegranates, burst as we savor them, word for word, phrase for phrase. The images explode with nuanced revelations! Lopez's magical touch renders these well-crafted poems into revelations of joy, sorrow, defiance and fierce presence. Brava, Jessica!

—**Norma E. Cantú**, *Norine R. and T. Frank Murchison
Distinguished Professor of the Humanities* at Trinity University;
Past President, The American Folklore Society; and Member of
the Conjunto de Nepantleras of the Esperanza Peace and Justice Center

Jessica Helen Lopez' voice is undeniably hers: strong and vulnerable, multi-lingual and verbose, a chanting and revolutionary cry. To read this work is to feel her voice erupt in your inner ear, to feel it waft over you like the burning of pitch from a furious torch held up against the darkening sky shouting its defiance, its willingness to be open, honest and weave a spell that makes you want to read more, to hear more, to be more. When I read these poems, I want to be more.

—**Don McIver**, *Basic Human Needs* Award Winning poet,
Host/producer of KUNM Afternoon Freeform; author of
The Noisy Pen and The Blank Page; and an editor of *A Bigger Boat:
The Unlikely Success of the Albuquerque Poetry Slam Scene*

These words are a journey through the tangled vines of the human heart, where every thorn and blossom serve as a testament to the dualities of existence—death and rebirth, pain and pleasure, sacrifice and renewal. These poems are an incantation. A ceremonial bloodletting. A lovely litany of libertad, invoking the indomitable.

—**Bobby LeFebre**,
Colorado Poet Laureate Emeritus

This collection is unrelenting in its strength and conviction. Jessica Helen Lopez shows us what it means to sing out of "lips [that] are like a thread of scarlet." These sleek and powerful poems teach us about untamable freedom as they dance and jump rope between lovers, mothers, and familial lineages. These poems will teach you the importance of existence as a revolution.

—**Tanaya Winder**, author of *Words Like Love*;
co-founder *As/Us: A Space for Women of the World*;
and founder of *Dream Warriors*

Jessica Helen Lopez brings the howling wind down from the mesas of Albuquerque, New Mexico like a revolutionary Adelita atop a wild mustang. Her verses of broken hearts and razorblades tucked in her trenzas gallop through your soul. More than a woman hollering, though, she laments the heart "falling away after its purpose is finished" like the fallen crimson fruit she names in her title. But her resilience overcomes the dark traumas of family disappointment and "the pinche SCOTUS [who] overturned Roe Vs. Wade". These poems are exquisite and dangerous at the same time. With each line Jessica Helen Lopez's voice sings true and visceral, gripping your heart and taking a bite.

—**Paul S. Flores**, San Francisco, CA - HBO Def Poet;
author of *We Still Be: Poems and Performances*,
a 2024 American Book Award Winner

Like her desert hometown of Deming, Nuevo México, Jessica Helen Lopez's poems are for the survivors; those who can flourish & bloom despite the scorching heat, droughts, & struggles along the borderlands. They are poems for the strong. On the page, she sculpts imagery that invokes the sacred, the political, & the personal. As a poet on the stage, Jessica commands the audience with fluid vocality, range, & presence like that of an actress. Her craft refines & reflects all of herself: la feminista, la revoluciónaria, la madre, la hija, la humanista. Her verses float between the written worlds of English y Español, as does she; between the worlds of the working class & the academic, as does she; between the worlds of the flesh & the spirit. As both Poet Laureate & National Poetry Slam Champion, Jessica Helen Lopez transcends all borders & labels that fail to define her; *My Heart is a Pomegranate, Mi Corazón es una Granada*, is testament. She is more. Her poems are more. She is la acequia amidst the seemingly endless badlands of Southern New Mexico. Her poetry is la agua to fill the mouths of those who need it most, at the very moment they need it most.

—**Damien Flores**, author of *Junkyard Dogs*;
National Poetry Slam Champion; host of
The Spoken Word Hour on 89.9 KUNM-FM

Jessica Helen López's poems are at once explosive and intimate, cries for justice and windows on a woman's life. They are powerful and true.

—**Margaret Randall**, poet, activist, author of over 150 books; recipient of the 2020 George Garrett Award for Outstanding Community Service in Literature presented by the Association of Writers and Writing Programs (AWP)

If Bukowski roared back into life as a long-tressed wild hearted woman who spilled the lousy whiskey of leering borrachos, he/she might be Jessica Helen Lopez. A defiant voice of Burque fire and wind and all that makes this high desert bloom! Poetry is the song sung by the wind, the bird and the silenced folk whose voice is of multitudes. Lopez writes and sings in that wind, that flight, that voice! Grand poetry! This book is her latest wild song, enjoy.

—**Bill Nevins**, poet and journalist; Chair of the Poetry & Film Chapter, New Mexico State Film Society; and Curator Director of the Santa Fe Poetry & Film Experience at the annual Santa Fe Film Festival

You may have heard it said that 'the heart is an open wound.' Welp, you haven't heard it read (nor said) like this. Jessica Helen Lopez says it. The thing. In a way that hurts and heals and howls and hungers and hopes. These are NOT words leaping off the page. These are words inked into your skin. These words sweat and chill and spill and drool and occasionally splatter (bring your own bib). Jessica reminds us that the heart is also a closed fist. A people's pump. A purple piston. A pregnant pistol. And when she is aiming hers at you ... you will listen and you'll remember.

—**Hakim Bellamy**, Inaugural Poet Laureate of Albuquerque and John F. Kennedy Center for the Arts Citizen Artist Fellow

Every so often, one reads, or listens, to a poet that allows everything around you - the pain, rage, sadness, fear, the leaving, the loss - to feel like it has a higher purpose than to weigh us down. Jessica is that poet. She writes, "...Forever righteous with rage, and no one will tell me otherwise." Then we are given permission, and invited, to harness the fires that are trying to burn us and use those fires as a torch during the dark. This poet's words and spirit is nothing short of a field of pomegranate trees in full bloom inviting us to hold its fruit like one holds the hand of a lover.

—**Alejandro Jimenez,** author of
There Will Be Days, Brown Boy (Mouthfeel Press)
and *Moreno. Prieto. Brown.* (Cafe con Libros Press)

One night, my friend and I were stumbling down Central Avenue when we heard words, pouring out of a café. There was Jessica Helen Lopez on the mic, reading a poem. Suddenly and I will never know how she conjured this- we turned into two yapping Chihuahuas, in the basket of her bicycle, she was pedaling fast. The Wicked Witch of the West? Light filtered through the cottonwood trees, first golden noon, then midnight silver. Her friend Brooke threw back her head (also on the bike) howling, La Llorona. We felt icy fingers on our little doggy necks. Just as suddenly, we were back in the Café, the whole audience ordering Sopapillas. Jessica led us in chanting "Tia! Tia! Sopapillas!" The warm, billowing pillows melted the honey. We were humans again and savored the deliciousness. If you are lucky, she will take you to the river on her bike and help you answer the eternal question. Your answer will be Christmas. It is always Christmas time with her. Jessica Helen Lopez is that good a poet.

—**Gary Max Glazner**, writer; founder of the Alzheimer's Poetry Project;
recipient of the 2013 Rosalinde Gilbert Innovations
in Alzheimer's Disease Caregiving Legacy Award;
and former Director of the Bowery Poetry Club of New York

My Heart is a
Pomegranate

Mi Corazón es una Granada

FLOWERSONG
PRESS

poetry by

Jessica Helen Lopez

FLOWERSONG
PRESS

FlowerSong Press
Copyright © 2024 by Jessica Helen Lopez
ISBN: 978-1-963245-48-6

Published by FlowerSong Press
in the United States of America.
www.flowersongpress.com

Cover Image by Jessica Helen Lopez
Author Image by Jessica Helen Lopez
Set in Adobe Garamond Pro

NOTICE: SCHOOLS AND BUSINESSES
FlowerSong Press offers copies of this book at quantity discount with bulk
purchase for educational, business, or sales promotional use. For information,
please email the Publisher at info@flowersongpress.com.

table of contents

My Heart is a
Pomegranate

Mi Corazón es una Granada

And I Told My Battered Mother that I am a Wild Horse Woman

Lodestar of the navigated unstrapped horse, but no I am not
a star. Haunches. Haunches of fire, I am, and he dared to call me, *bitch*.
If I was a female dog in heat, how he would know it by my bite.

My mother, battle weary woman of battering, still married to
the bastard I call father asks, *Are you going to be okay?*

I don't fault her that she is unfamiliar with my unbridled surge,
my thigh-heavy power of a muscled ability to run. Gallop. Galvanize. Gloat.

She never learned

how to leave, lurch, lean into a wild dark froth, frenzied freedom. I have been
practicing for years. Penultimate fleeing of the long-maned unfettered filly.

He called me *bitch, punk, asshole, jerk.* And I yanked myself
from his crooked story that was not my own. Cycle breaker.

Breaker of cycles, I am. Lodestar gazer of the untamed equine. I have
been running with and from wolves since the day I was bore,

glistening, black sweaty coat cut from my mother's gut.
I escaped you, your husband, *him,* long before any of you noticed.

I am sleek like that. I am powerful beyond
all of your imaginations, like that.
Like that, I am a stealth, steely, wild mustang,
like that.

Mestengo. Mostrenco.
Masterless cattle.

I do not revivify your long and dark traumas.
I will not be beaten, whupped, worn down.

I'd rather die a mighty death, unmountable mare,
before I ever let you

or you or you whip me to a filigree.

Witness my froth, foam and gloating teeth. See how I gleam,
gloam in the darkness, horse body like a locomotive sweeping
the wind and bullet-fast into the plains of tall grass, slicing the night
into a soundless, furious tune.

I am wild, like that.
Untamable, like that.
Like that, I am free.

See, how I buck you from this body I was beholden to? This body
that neither belongs to you or you or you or *him*. It is mine and mine

alone, dark horse of the underdog, brimstone and feral as fuck.

I am more than okay, mother. I am the mare, the stallion and the herd.
I am the herd in lust with the lodestar, the ever guiding light
into the great and wild darkness.

Forever righteous with rage, and no one
will tell me otherwise

My Heart is a Pomegranate

*Once when I was living in the heart of a pomegranate, I heard a seed
saying, "Someday I shall become a tree, and the wind will sing in
my branches, and the sun will dance on my leaves, and I shall be
strong and beautiful through all the seasons."*

—*The Pomegranate, Khalil Gibran.*

O' crown of the mouth of an organic trumpet.
O' stolen fruit of the next-door neighbor's bush.
O' *granada de sangre de cristo y pietá de las lágrimas.*
O' piston of sex and unshaved legs. Pouty lips.
O' russet-hued skin of the deciduous, immature plummet of *la fruta.*

We are the falling away after its purpose is finished.
We are the dropping of a part that is no longer needed or useful.

O' seedy gory guts of the bleeding, sliced open intestines of the pomegranate.
O' heart of mine, acidic strangeness, astringent plaything, chambers of a red drum.

O' tumult.
O' unheard wrath.
O' tiny disaster and tsunami of peel and pulp.
O' sad syrup of the crimson saliva swirled between
and made from the molasses of our mouths.

We are the underworld, fruit of the dead sprung from the blood of Adonis.
We are Persephone's long winter, bride of Hades counting the abacus of time.
We are Zapata's assassination, spilled veins of *El Caudillo del Sur.*
Heart of the peasants.

O' death-dealing, poppy-pods of the left breast.
O' contradiction of little lies spout from the right.
O' Our Lady of the Pomegranate, fertility and boiled wheat.

My heart is a pomegranate again, bloody open mouth
of meat and fruit, a million tiny seductive seeds –
orbs of myopic clustered eyes.

Orb of the everlasting calyx red bell rising, ringing with a gelatinous love
that flowers nowhere. Nomadic and without root.

O' Holy of the Holies and Solomon sings,

Thy lips are like a thread of scarlet, and thy speech is comely:
thy temples are like a piece of a pomegranate within thy locks.

Chisel

A Story of Cycling, Confession and Hope

(How a woman finally fled her abusive intimate domestic partner)

The cirrus clouds are chiseled from a weepy
gray sky, and down comes the water. Teary
globe-shaped droplets fashioned from dust,
atmospheric smoke. It is raining on me,
wetness pooling at the visor of my white
hand-me-down bicycle helmet. I pedal.
Watch with one right upward eye as the rain,
drop-by-drop, one-by-one gathers, flicks into vision.
Suspended, glorious fat plop-by-plop, flees
my peripheral, loosened wet smattering into
the receding southward winds.

I feel like a God.

It brings me peace, though also a sweet
alarm that I may crash my bike
into the coolness of a slick street,
any given moment. I am 25 miles into it,
clocking 24.2 mph downhill. I am flying. I am
beyond redemption. I am toe-soaked and shivering,
sweaty conundrum. I am hot and cold. 26 miles
into my journey. My wristbound GPS clocks 44
years, on the cusp of 45 years into this life.
I am old and young.

Piston pump. The sprocket springs to action,
shifts a greased derailleur. Chain. Cable. Slope
of the tube. Sacred geometry, bible of the golden
ratio, oily slide of perpetual motion. I am neither
simile or metaphor. I am hyperbole
readied for crash.
I think of Da Vinci's elegant failure

in achieving never-ending
happiness, a frictionless frenzy.
He wrote that,

sound equates to energy loss,

and my lungs
are billowing sails, blowhards.

Noisy. Erratic. Loud living things.
Struggling gills. Entropic
fools of this physical world.

My silence cannot feed me.
I cannot carry these year-long secrets.
So, I breathe and lean into the
mean hardness of truth. I write and ride
garishly now, daring him or you
to contradict that which is true.

You. You. You.
Abused me and abused
her, too.

Mathematical, savage brute.
I am ostentatious truth of this
rain-soaked afternoon and the water
is a balm, medicine to break me loose.

Kali, of the darkened flooded blue.
Kali, of the darkened flooded blue.

This, how I ride a bike.
I am the beautiful mistake. Basquiat's
overdose. A serendipitous swan dive and
dove tail.

Still I ride. 27 miles,
43.4523 kilometers

of vertiginous,
pleasurable
pain.

Because it hurts the lungs,
is why I ride.

It is raining hard now and still I pedal, pencil-thin
long-legged centrifugal pump. Chimney Jack.
Roasting skewer over fire. I will ride until I die.
Hyperglide and a mouth full of teeth dancing
in-lock, two-step and fancy-footed drive train.

28 miles and I think that my bones have melded
into the *horsebody* of my aluminum steed. I whinny.
Neigh. Kick back asphalt and grind the glossy
street. Amalgamate. Mercurial me. I used to think
I was weak. Still do, here and there.
But, in this clocking minute,
RPM spindle Chisel of the wet cloud,
I am a specialized stumpjumper. A baby hop.
A miniature wild bunny. A tailwhip of the Mind,
muddied minefield. Manic Maxis XC machine
stomping, walking in my big black boots.
A strutting peacock plumage, king of the pen.
Queen of the roost.

I dream
in Mezzotint.
I am neither stipple nor crosshatch.
I am pure slinky, slippery ink. Indigo on wheels.
Story on paper. Tar of the Gutenberg font. Tire track
and hieroglyphic Cave of Lascaux. I leave my story
folded into the Hero Dirt of a left-behind relationship
with Death itself. O' how he romanced the stone.
No longer. I prefer to be alone upon
this body of a two-wheeled pegasus
meant for me and me alone.
My dedicated atonement.

9

I am the ruckus, leaving behind the rubbage,
the salt-soaked tears of a rainy desert sky, and lies
and no love lost. For there was no love to begin with.

I imagine I am royal as I whirl around my city,
rain-drenched though common-as-fuck. Discount
sneaker-footed rotating gyroscopes clocking mileage.

I am sloppy when I ride my bike.
Chaos and composition.
I am the contradiction,
a learned and unlearned beastly thing.

Still I ride,

29 miles and then 30 and there goes 31

     s   t   r   e   t   c   h   i   n   g

            s   t   r   e   t   c   h   i   n   g

                        s   t   r   e   t   c   h   i   n   g

into a long winded 1720 cache yards and I become
human again. Rotors spinning like silvery orbs loosening
their light, again. Baby girl, breathing again. Letting go
the fist and hammer again. Ending and starting over again.

Calipers pinching, pausing, feathering. This finger.
That finger, black triangle of tubes pulling.
I am middle-aged again. I am my own woman again.
I am without a man again, heavy-handed, live-wire
secretive, behind-closed-doors violence. Again. Emboldened
by faith and freedom again and I don't care who knows.

Even him. Even him.

I am Daedulus's warning, beeswax warming.

The sparrow's last flight of Icarus.
I am the V2 29 622 X 30 width of the rim.
Fixed point of the center.

Slowing.
Fatigued.
Finished.

The hunted and the prey.
The feral felled.
The slain and Lady Lazurus rising.
The victim and survivor.
The powerless and the powerful.

I am both old and young. Both dumb and wise.
I am both loved and unloved. Both happy and
melancholia drowning. I am both motion
and non-motion. Both slow and fast,
and who gives a fuck? Ain't no one
watching, hawk-eye critiquing,
cussing, spitting, insulting
hollering at me, no more.

No more.
No more.

I am wettened wind in the hair,
perfectly flawed and flawless.

I am unfree and both free.
Fixed and both infinite.
The banished and the banisher.

I forget to remember. I remember to forget.

I am both the breath and the un-breath.
I am the chisel.
I am the clay.

I am riding my bike in the rain.
It is the first day of Spring.

It is raining and I am
riding my bike in the rain.

My loneliness, that
relentless
long snake
of a train,

abated,
wettened,

in
love
with

riding my
bike in

the rain.

I Pour Whiskey On Him

after Bukowski

but the bluebird only sings louder,
warbles drunk on a barstool, swivel-stupid
dizzy with love or the lie of love

I say *stay in there blue bird, stay*
inside my crooked too-skinny shitty
little chest,
but here it comes, slanted
singing sloppy, chirping

tunes to scare away the men
who don't like blue birds, who are
afraid of the blue and how the blue
is deep and deafening

so I pour more whiskey on its wings, strike
a phosphorous match and it lights up
like a fucking torch, now it is a phoenix,
an orange and yellow blazing house fire, a furnace
alit in my chest right there in front of all the other

borrachos at the bar who are hoping to score, fuck
somebody, anybody who agrees to go home
with them, to pretend at love
and flying and singing until

the dawn drums its way into morning, and
then they kick the blue bird out of their bed
into the asphalt-lined street to fend for its own

Blue bird, be still, I say. *Don't move or make a sound,*
trick the would-be and wannabe lovers into
into thinking you don't exist

they don't want to know that you exist, anyways
anyways, don't weep little blue bird
don't show them your little
blue bird tears

Trenzas

A poem for the Tiguex Park Rally in Burque, Nuevo México
on the day that the pinche SCOTUS overturned Roe V Wade.

Really, slick licorice sticks catching the light like an oil puddle mid-afternoon.
Really, two long licks of dynamite, fuse-fury, flammable and the sizzle of sulfur.
Really, a pair of woven braids, sweet grass flying in the wind like two dizzy kites

as I ride my hand-me-down bike, fast-footed,
and crazy-legged
into a desert sunset.

Really, birds cooing like lovers.
Really, lovers slicing their wicked little wrists.
Really, piecemealed stories, ritual, ceremony, grandmother's dead
daughter, mama's laughter, daddy's anger and last night's neon-lit sins.

Really, tears. Wet, slick watery *saltspit* of the duct. Sobbing.
Really, sobbing like *Chavela's* last drunken sorrowful song and bar-brawl.
Really, also the backhanded wood paddle brush of my auntie *thump, thump,*
thumping my head because I won't sit still.

Really, the scalp pulled so tight you can't see straight for a week.
Really, the way my daddy used to wind bits of leather and feather into *mis pelos,*
before he decided he was bored of me and never touched my hair again.

Really, *blackblackblack* in the winter.
Really, *redbrownredbrown*, a bit o' gold in the summer.

Really, short. Really, long.
Really, *trenzas* like a noose, like a jump rope, like a live wire,
like red, green and white yarn.
Trenzas con la bandera de México.

Really, *trenzas* like *Adelita,*
soldaderas y *maquiladoras,*
the left-behind women,

the sisters, daughters, wives,
cooks, maids, sweat-drenched braids
of garment factory seamstresses.
Like revolution, love,
rape, and rage.

Like how *Villa* took his women, slippery
sliding between his fingers.

Trenzas like blood.
Trenzas like sugar.
Trenzas like hunger.

Trenzas like *pan dulce,*
trenzas de brioche,
trenzas de
arroz con leche,
almonds, walnuts and the sweet, rich,
body of fig, figment and raisin.

Trenzas de glaseadas
de crema
frutos secos.

Trenzas like, *¿Quieres chingasos, guey?*

I've tucked a razor blade into my left trenza,
a silver bullet sleeps in my right.
I'm hiding an entwined secret
in the lace and lattice of my hair,
my braid, my breast, my milk,

my meat, my life, my death,
my birthing, my abortion,

my abortion,
my abortion,
my abortion,

my lust, my revenge.
The rope of my womanhood,

blood in my hair, blood in the teeth
of the comb, blood of the ribbon and bow,
yoke and harness. *Xochitlquetzal -*
flower, flower, flower of desire.

Trenzas.
Trenzas.
Trenzas.

Trenzas.
Trenzas.
Trenzas.

Mis trenzas sin vergüenza.

Realmente,
mis trenzas son preciosas
y malvadas.

Mis trenzas te
ahogarán hasta
la muerte.

For the Boys Bumping Kendrick

The morning after yet another school mass shooting and with respect to virtuoso rap lyricist Kendrick Lamar, recipient of the Pulitzer Prize for distinguished musical composition.

Loyalty was the word of the day, fat booty bass
oozing from their four-door matte black Tacoma
truck spilling out and into the sunny autumnal
afternoon all over Central Avenue. Their smiles
were a collection of 5000 Lumen LED light bulbs
bobbing and weaving with a good time, necks
swiveling and everyone of them wore their
seatbelts like their mamas taught 'em.

Their *happy* was infectious, ya'll and I caught it,
thumping in the middle of my chest as I saddled
my dusty red Jeep Wrangler next to their truck
on the corner of
Somewhere and *That Place*.

The traffic light, was a big red halting hand telling
the world to sit still, for at least a little while.
I'm an old lady by their standards, but they waved
when they saw how I head-nodded and mouthed
the words, *Kung Fu Kenny*.

Today the morning news reported four dead bodies,
children shot up by another child while they sat at their desks
pumping out arithmetic and iambic pentameter or maybe, merely
just watching a wistful sun arc across a grease smeared school window,
bored chins propped by hands, eyes that averted the scribble-scrabble
of whiteboard, ears that muffled the teacher's drone.

Or perhaps they thought about college or sex or about
how their fathers and mothers can't afford the rent, but mostly
they probably just thrummed with the energy of their youth,
young brains churning with whatever young thoughts they churned.

And then a deep low bass, or was it a rattle
of bullets like a snare drum? I can't remember
what the reporter reported about what type of gun

the boy used to squeeze a shower of lead from
and into the soft, surprised bodies of his classmates.
But he shot them dead. And this afternoon,

they are still dead. And dead forever they will remain,
crystallized in their youth, never to graduate,

get a job, lose a job, fall in love,
get divorced, raise a dog, lose a dog,
go bankrupt,
pay their first mortgage,
travel to India or Guatemala,
seek therapy for their mid-life crises,
ring in another new year.

Sing along to their favorite song.

Kendrick says *shimmy-yeah, shimmy-yeah,*
shimmy-yeah rock and he says,
done been down so long, lost hope
done came down so hard I slowed.

The boys were bright and alive
and happy to breathe, to shine
and shout together in unity,
loyalty, loyalty, loyalty.

The light turned green
and off they drove
with a wave and not
a care in the world.

Cool as cool teenagers can be,
seven off to the Golden Shovel.

Prolly' playing hooky.
I was so glad for them, so
grateful for their beautiful,
boyish buoyancy
that I almost cried.

My chest felt 'bout to burst,
spilling open all of my joy
out and onto the dashboard.

Right there, on the corner
of *Somewhere* and *That Place*.

They drove off with a wave.

Fridamania

Frida this and Frida that. Warhol Frida. Pixelated Frida.
Frida wearing The Cure T-Shirt. Frida grabbing her cunt.
Frida holding a baby. Frida and Marylin Monroe.
Frida on the cover of Vogue. Selma Hayek is Frida.
Madonna was not. Frida posters. Frida pillows.
Fu Lang Chang and I. 1937 wooly-haired child.

Frida Gone Wild. Frida car seat cover, salt
and pepper shakers. Frida soap. Frida keyrings.
Frida shirts and skirts and Frida phone cases.
Frida is at the swap meet and Frida was once at Walmart.
They turned Frida into a velvet painting of a cat with tits.

Frida is a lightswitch cover and Frida is a mouse pad.
That chick down the street dressed up as Frida for Halloween.
Actually, I counted at least three Fridas that year. I even saw
a blonde haired, North East Heights Frida hanging out
with *El Muerte Pelon*.

He did not get the memo that *Dia de los Muertos*
ain't Hallows's Eve.
But sometimes white people be like that.

Frida was Indigenous until she was not.
Frida was nationalist until she was not.
Frida was a Communist. Frida was not elite until she was.
Frida ate the bourgeois for dinner and then hung her paintings
across the Paris skyline. New York too. Frida snubbed the *pinche* galleries.

Frida is romanticized revolution. They cremated Frida when she died.
Frida is a clay urn. Frida is hammer and sickle. Frida is a celebrity.
Diego swallowed some of Frida's ashes. This is how he choked on guilt.

Frida is a *puta*. Frida doesn't give a shit. Frida don't care about
your analytical essays and academic interpretations. Frida does

not know that she is a calendar, coaster, book bag or sweatshirt.
Frida is glad that she is dead. Frida is stitched in a third-world country
sweat shop, sold discount at the corner *Fallas Super Store.*

Frida was high class. Frida appropriated. Frida's first love was
named Alejandro. Frida fucked. A lot. Frida was a man. Frida
smoked finger-rolled cigarettes. Drank like a fish.
Knew she would die. We all die.

Frida knew Pablo Picasso. Frida was not one Frida, Frida
was *Dos Fridas.* Frida was sexy and she knew it. So, what?
Frida fucked Leon Trotsky and Josephine Baker. So, what?

Frida was not *Tehuantepec.* Frida didn't care. Frida, Frida,
Frida, fetishized. Frida made money. Frida did not care.
Frida was cosmopolitan. Frida did not beg on the streets.
Frida always had food and paint and never had to worry
how to pay to get drunk. Frida was social capital and clout.

Frida is commodification at its best. Frida is painted gold.
Frida is rendered and dismembered. Frida is fractured.
Frida was young when she died old.
Did Frida fuck O'Keefe? Who knows? So, what?

Frida and Chavela fell in love. Frida and Dolores del Rio did not.
The symbol for sin and the devil is the monkey.
Two Nudes Sit in the Forest. In 2016, Christie's sold it for 8 million
ice cold dollars. Frida did not see a dime. She was dead.

Madonna tried to buy it but was outbid. Frida is a joke
with a punchline we don't get. Frida is a blockbuster movie.
She is an Etsy custom die-cut sticker made by Karen
who used to work at the mall but now reads tea leaves and is an artist.

Frida was not deported. Frida did not cross the border.
Frida did not ride *El Tren de la Muerte* and Frida *es sin
papeles.* Frida was never deloused or sat shotgun in a lowrider,
Bel-Air 58 Sparkle, high in the sauce.
Frida is a *piñata.* They beat her with sticks until her candy falls out,
and it does, fall out. Showers us with rainbow-trout

iridescent hued, cellophane-covered *dulce, dulce, dulce.*
The kind that gives you cavities.
So sweet that you never want to wash
the taste from your mouth.

Ode to Velour Roses, War and the Survival of My Divorce

Sweet light of the earth, wee rose
crimson star of the scarlet letter, bloom
of the desert dirt, cinnamon dust and silt
slippery as Christ's last day on earth,

Shroud of Turin.

You rise from winter's slumber blooming bold,
skirt of the ruffled petticoat, perennial flower
of rosacea, redblot and last season's love.

Superior ovary of botany, reminds me that spring *is* here,
was not lost in the tide of the white, winter blindness.

I survived my *swansongmarriage*. I survived.
Then, six months, almost seven of a deep-rooted sleep.

Though I survived
years of the hollow.
Comatose, but not
death after all. Chrysalis hiding.
Busy with subterranean magic.

Twirling. Tilling. Toil of the new twilight.
Crepuscular, muscled and primal.
Ancestor of the *Rosa Gallica*, medicine
maker. Velvet crimson glory.

You moved towards the hip seed
in the smallest of increments, a pace
almost made of nothing.

I am your most patient nurse.

I smell the blossoms.

Parthian war.
Persian flirt.

Large and showy, prickle of red, stain of a clotted
blood. How you gloat in the sunset, alive
with an arrogant fire. Conceited as fuck,
but regal and you know it. Little queens of the thorn,
stalks of long neck. Imperial regalia
of orb and scepter.

One bush. Two bush. *Birthheavy.* Bashful at first, then
a full fire. A raging light. Green of the five-leaflet
wove in chlorophyll and anatomy of miracle. Sizzling
with sun, awash in moon, quenched by jilted rains and the tender
garden hose feeding your mycelium, body fuel and busy little fungi.

Stipule. Petiole. Lusty floral and fauna,
braggadocious, dripping with your sex.
Bordeaux. Cardinal. Claret.
Red wine stain on a white blouse.
Pouty mouth. Glamorous garnet.

Gleaming. Gilded.
Imploding potpourri.
Sateen sprout of
the sticky knotted pistil.

This one, then that one.
Then this one. That one. This one.
Then dozens and dozens. Buds imploding,
popping into existence.

Like a slash of red, you slice open the day.
Manifold of morphology. Sun-hatched bloody
little bombs of beauty.

I marvel at your glittering resilience to return.
The way you war your way back to existence,
fragile rage and restoration of a *holy, holy spring.*
Perfume drunk. I am perfume drunk with my little power.

A necromancer calling forth the floriculture of my front yard
rosebeds. I prune. Pour horseshit into the pockets of my patch
of earth, beckon the flowers to *riseriserise* from the long darkness.

I am the conductor and you
my best seasonal symphony, ascending
scale of frequency, thrumming with a silent growing pitch.

I am drunk with an ancient knowledge
only those who cheat death
know, only those who have tended to their grief
as one does a beloved garden.

The lip of the rose
is the softest flesh I know,

but I,

I have gone to war and returned a fist.
It is rich and good, after all.

Shit For the Roses

Little brother with a shock of black thick hair, jutting from his small head,
this way, that way, a rampant onyx bush on fire emanating flames of follicle
from his too-fertile skull, housing his muddied but beautiful and flawed brain,
his cancered scalp, his alcoholic forest of breath and forced lungs, the DTs quaking
through his nerves and nerve endings. One. Two. Three. The intubator shoves puffs
of oxygen into his lungs of fluid. He developed pneumonia this morning. He is swimming
in his own water. His feet are filthy. His toenails curved scythes, banged up and bruised shins.

He falls a lot when he is drunk, which is all of the time.
My brother is a map of contusions.

His feet are that of a wild animal, maybe coyote, maybe badger. Puffed out veins
stuffed with benzos and the names of sedatives that I cannot pronounce. He shits
in a bag. A long flattened tube winding from his anus and despite the smell, it is
pretty. His shit is a mossy green clay, soft like a baby's excrement. Milk-fed and
liquid. Little brother of the veil of black thick eyelashes, swollen shut. He has not
seen, with his eyes, this world for five days. But he sees, and I wonder what he
dreams in that shifting plumage of man-made coma. And the busy-bee team of
doctors and nurses poke his arms, fluff his pillows, drain his trachea, pump him
full of Ativan and Fentanal and potassium, carelessly saving his life.

For if he does die, will they care? Do they think of my brother when they vacate
their zombie-eyed, twelve-hour shifts? While they drive home, eat their dinners,
take their showers, water their cucumber gardens? Have their marital affairs and
pet their cats?

*The ICU ward is a bramble of sounds colliding; the soft padding of nurses' feet,
hospital pudding and trays clinking, the hushed words of a foxhole prayer, bleeping
and blipping and whooshes and dings, grandmothers' weeping, the Price is Right and
the Days of Our Lives jingles wafting in low audible tones from televisions floating
above beds, the shifting of stiff white sheets, coughs, farts, moans, cursing, crying and
more crying, and that one visiting, endearing uncle laughing and talking too loud. It
is devoid of any scent other than ethyl and isopropyl sterilizing alcohol and shit. You
can smell the shit. The body has a way of rising to the surface.*

Back at home, I tend my front yard roses. The petals are swollen with a beautiful
rage. It is the rot, the owner and the slave. O' soft and salacious bloom. This is

what I say to myself as I pour my love into the earth: *Brother, throw the sateen body of your animal self from a cliff.* Don't return and keep the story of our childhood from forming upon your lips. Don't let it spill into the soil. And so, little brother, I too, don't let a single word slip into the mud. I keep these words to myself, never to be spoken aloud. This is how I guard our shared memories locked into the daring and tragic bud.

I water our shared big sister and little brother lives, prune the extraneous leaves from the stalk. I avoid the thorns. I know why you drink your life away, but I won't tell, little brother. Not while our parents still live. They are afraid of their high-noon shadows, how it will eat them alive. They cannot grow from the slurry of their own making. I know why you drink the way you do, flirting with your blackout death. The way you do.

Wake up, little brother. Or don't. Wake your grown-man, almost-forty-year-old body, (or don't) so I can look into your eyes once more. Even if to bid a final farewell. Say without words that we share of the feast of the same garden. Don't wake, little brother. Don't wake and I won't blame you if you do. Or don't.

Wild, untamed, hurting, hopeful, and fed by the shameful shit
of our flawed parents' manure. That which gave us life despite it all.

My roses are bountiful this season. Little brother, and if you do wake, I will bring you a bushel. I will bring you a vase cut from hard, glittering glass, brimming with a riotous explosion of their colors. They are growing, living, thirsty as you are for the elixir that brings them life. We are drunk on the petal of the wine.

Though, little brother, unlike you, they thrive and throb with a dark, sweet rot. They live and die, only to live again. They turn that shit into gold.

Marquez, Neruda and the First Time You Made Language Out Of Love

If nothing saves us from death, at least love should save us from life.
—Pablo Neruda

My light released like an ingot of pure and pale white
juice spurt of the fleshy fruit plunged by hungry teeth.
A bird flew from a branch that grew from my scalp,
and it ate of the plum tree that grew from yours.

This was its great escape and thunderous relief.

Knowing that food can always be found elsewhere,
still it feasted from this place. This place where our
knees touch and the gardens of our bodies produce sweat.

The night became amaranthine,
became the sugar of a hot moon.

I am the flame licking the long copper skin,
you are the eyes of a blue dog. Together
we are two wings of a nesting hen.

Mountain Bike Trail, Baby Wheelies and
the Rio Grande

I love you and so I followed you into the wild, my
bike chain squeaking and I did not know what gear to stay in.
The cranes were soft-white, 10-watt halogen bulbs,
skimming the shallow winter river, spindled-
scavengers of the wetland, gregarious bird of Alaska,
Siberia, too. I wanted to sound smart and so I mused aloud,
They must be eating grubs and look there are 13 of them.
Together they are called a dance. Herd of the Sandhill,
long necks. *They are majestic party favors, silent but festive*
festooned with a quiet, stolid beauty. You turned to me and I saw the sun
setting in your eyes. How alive you were. I should have been more
excited than I was, but the gold glint of the Rio Grande
lulled me and I was unusually calm. When you kissed
me your lips were cold and wet, our clunky bike helmets
head-butted one another sounding a lovely, awkward
 muted thunk.

I laughed and the moment shifted,
as moments do.

I kept up with you,
followed the winding trail perched atop my refurbished
front-wheel, shock-absorbent hardtail bike. I was not surprised
at my agility, for I am young in the heart and in the thighs.

I popped a tiny wheelie, emulating your grand
mountain bike skills
and felt proud, as if I was
your daughter or maybe a best friend.

You rode into the wind,
slicing it neatly with your lean body,
black matte bike with all of its impressive gadgets.
You pumped your legs and the chambers of your heart,

exalting that thing called life.
You were as gorgeous as a gilded bell.

The blood rushed to the crown of your brown
cheeks coloring you russet,
cold wind-whipped nose and mouth
the hue of a clay jug.

You were a benevolent and patient teacher,
and my admiration of you was a new and wisened
glowing, growing respect.

I knew then I would love you for always.

The cranes kept at their eating, pecking mealy plants,
grains and miniature crustacean of prey.

Long-legged luminescent creatures, overstaying
their migration, a late November surprise.

They became smaller and smaller in the distant past,
as we created miles between us and them.

We thrust our childlike, jocular legs like pistons,
the tread beneath us imprinting a lattice into the dirt,
delicate like the fossil of an ancient fern or a sand-colored lace.

The river told me that you loved me, too.
But I don't think you heard its gurgling secret.
You rode ahead, turned a corner,
cottonwood and dead tree, dark bark
enveloping your shadowy shape
and I lost sight of you.

For a good two minutes or three, I lost sight of you.
Breathlessly, I was alone and it felt good and cold in my bones.
I can't remember if I was sad.

I trilled with the delicious thought
that I could become lost, thick in the dying forest,

the braided brush, home of horsetail, fragrant
ash, salt grass,
left behind never to catch up
to you.

Always a few yards behind.
Lost like how I am used to,
a comfortable, comforting
aloneness.

Orson wrote that we are born into this world
solo and that is how we shall leave it.

No matter, the cranes are etched into
the gelatin silver-plated photo of that day,
and they always come back.

Maybe they never left.

The White Burro

This poem is not about the brown horse.
It is not about love or his glimmering skin, my
lover, and it is not about the brown horse penned
alongside the Bosque acre, swimming long-legged
and knobby-kneed among the thin blades of
tall grass growing lush despite the unseasonably hot summer.
It is not about how the brown horse scoffed at my advances,
my clicking tongue, my lusty chittering mouth sounds
or how the sky melted like a sweet orange and pink
creamsicle above our heads, a popsicle letting loose
its atoms and chemical colors, cumulus clouds
loftily lollying about the sky as we gazed from
the bike trail, 40 or 50 yards away, two shimmering
five-fingered humans in love with ourselves more
than with each other.

This poem is not about the brown horse, majestic being
that it was, rather, it is about the fat-bellied white burro.
That friendly companion, pack animal of the working class,
beast of burden, and how it nudged alongside the featherless pegasus
body of the brown equine, caring less if it was more beautiful than the next.

Who cared? Not in the least the white, gray-hued burro, big-headed
cunny arse and pack-mule for the connoisseur of Dionysus's best wine.
This poem is not about the brown horse. It is about the white burro, dusty
with a tinted watercolor grayness, who begrudgingly came to the edge of that
length of ranchero, rustic rabbit fence and neighed lightly, and with black
bulging eyes on each side of his thick white head,
accommodated my need for love when I beckoned him.

Maybe a Jack. Maybe a Jenny. Him/Her. Though, I will say again, this poem
is not about the brown horse. It is a poem about how that mostly
white burro jejune with a grayness, chewed cud side by side the
sable-soft brown horse, standing there in the middle of that fenced off
acre of green, green wispy foliage of Mexican feather grass. It is a poem
about how that milk-sud burrow sauntered over, a lazy bored

king of behooved giants and thick rind of protruding belly, then bowed his
head like a modest, humbled servant of servants, and how he walked
towards us and how he thrust his fat-barrelled moist nose, nostrils
like bottomless caves between the linked
man-made fence. He made us his friend.

I liked it more than he knew, that nonchalant burro, and more than he knew,
my lover sitting atop his specialized mechanical mountain bike, black helmet
shining beneath a dwindling desert sun, glowing like a little boy holding a rose
and more than the brown horse, the burro's companion,
would ever know, too. I liked it the best. I liked the white, hoary stubble-
faced burro the best. Silently, I thanked every goddess and god
I ever knew for the blessing of that incomparable moment. We rode that late afternoon,

that early Summer desert evening, atop our mountain bikes
kicking up dust behind our fat tires and both he and I,
my lover and me, we stopped when we saw, from across the arroyo fed
by the waters of a beleaguered drought-riddled Rio Grande, a patch of
ornamental grass waving at us in the wind housing two souls; one, a sooty
bay brown babe, the other a squat winter white braying donkey.

Of the two, only one was friendly with the idea of love. We called to them,
the brown horse and the white burro, perched up on our separate mechanisms
of mountain bikes, pausing our 12-mile ride, sweat tearing down our throats,
thirst parching the insides of our necks. The white burro beckoned, an eager
relative. The brown horse remained rigid in its beauty. I wrote a poem in my head.

He took a picture and asked, *Are you crying?* He was used to my sudden tears
sprout from the awe of beauty, life, love, pain, loss, grief, and the in-between.

I said, *I'm not crying.* The salt gathered and weeped from the inner corner of my
eyes. I lied as I weeped at the sight of the perfectly shaped odd four-legged friend,
white but also dusky, snuffled its nose between the chinks of the fence. So far
away, but closer than it was before, that white burro loved me and I loved that white
burro. The brown horse remained in the center of the field, untouched by our
human presence and I said aloud to my beloved that I will write a poem about
this gorgeous, strange white burro. I will. And he laughed, a deep round laugh,
launching his bike, forward and determined to use his brown body like a piston.
He left me behind, a dusty trail of desert dirt kicking up into the air. I remained for
one more moment. The white burro could care less that I was about to depart.

It had already turned its back to me, its thick ass and heavy haunches sauntering, making its way to the brown horse, standing in the middle of the grass like a statue.

Or a god.

Xipe Totec Ate the Obsidian Butterfly

And all of the medicine of the world was devoured, old
and young women alike, the before-birth female babies, two-
spirited ones. The bones of the clawed butterfly were ground
to white dust, chalk of air and blown into the wind, all seven
parts of the stars of the sky. No flesh to be flayed, for she never
owned the skin of the blood. *Xipe* kept her clavicle instead, wore
it like an instrument, a thin-stripped whistle around his neck.
Trophy of his triumph. Sharpened her left-handed pinky bone
to a whittle, and pierced his septum with it. He made an ornament
of her. This is how the men rid the jungles and forests of the women.

This is how he excised her and all of her to follow.
Who remembers her skeletal wings, black mirrors
of flight, burnished glass?

Reflection of the two-headed doe?
La gama of the spectrum.
Coneja pierced by the twelve spears.
Agamemnon's sacrificial daughter, slain stag
of Artemis and antlers of the moon.

Wing and bone. Bone and wing.
Velvet horn of the fawn-bearing bovine.
Ĩtzpāpālōtl of the many animal tribes,
hoof and float, wing heart of chitin.

Xipe Toltec, Asesino Nuestro Señor
de la Mariposa Desollada y Obsidiana.

Tzitzimitl. Star Demon.
She a sharpened tool,
he a guiltless mouth of guile,
of gnashing teeth,
brilliant and brutal, everlastingly
seduced by the white man's betrayal.
The world of earth animals, the two-legged peoples,
the four-legged walkers, the green plants,
all colors of the blossoms, Spider Woman's legs and thorax,

swollen womb of spiderlings, families of trees, all of our
winged relatives, the finned-bodies
of the swimming ones, pools of mouth-gaped salmon,
invertebrates of salt and the gushing water-atoms too, have
fallen, fallen into
the chasm of chaos.

He is the oil devouring the lakes.
He is the acid burn of the oceans.
He is the scorch of the leafy canopies.
He is the toppling of the red tent.
He is the Christian Christ, the President,
Pope, Tyrant, Swindling Dilettante and he
is the Pirate and the Parliament.

He eats.
He is eating.
He keeps eating and eating.
He ate the medicine and it is no more.

He is the flayed one who forgot the spring
and only remembers the gold.

& it is a round pretty thing

& i went outside to worship the wolf moon. every orb
i have looked upon has done good by me & this was no
exception, round pretty thing brimming of light & swollen
diaphanous moth wings. we all die and & I am no longer fearful
of my great retreat into that ether of ash & carbon. the moon
is a pacifier, round pretty thing. there are nights when I am
datura. jimsonweed. angel's trumpet. attracting sphinx
wooly dense tiger coat and pollinators too. blooming only
when the sun goes down. short-lived cereus. princess of the night.
christ in the manger. *dome de noche.* i divorced you last year
& fell in love with a new man. he gifts me potted orchids
& paintings. tells me i am beautiful & pens me poems.
cums hard into me & whispers lovemaking words that i
cannot decipher. he does not love me back, not really,
but this is fine & like the winter moon does
i am cradled by his calculated coldness. how
he hangs in the wind 75.8 degrees above the horizon.
a white dot against the black, black sky. &, yet, he does
me good. holds the space that you once occupied. the 13th
moon of the longest year of my life. an icy white orb, round
pretty thing. pregnant with distraction. he makes me forget
that one day i will die. & he makes me forget. you.

Scars

I have licked your scars with my generous tongue,
a catapult of *la lengua*, hot pink sensory organ of the mouth,
8,000 taste buds of umami, pulsing *sabor* of the receptor cell.

It is an impressive regeneration of collagen, your scars,
the wound repair of your body, bevy of lesions
fashioned from the fibrous gossamer of your netted tissue.
How they build themselves ziggurat, bold in the closure
of contusion, cuts, scrapes, road rash, rage and burn.
Jacob's Ladder of coiled twists and turns. Your body's glue.

You collect scars lovingly and tell me that scars are inevitable.
I admire your courage though I fear for you as a woman who
loves a man who courts
danger, does.

Your right shoulder dawns a star-struck, thick whitened, puffed
gathering of knotted skin, cross-hatch of reborn flesh, fortuna
for the muscle of my tongue to flick, fondle, finger.

I open my red-hot, blood-juiced mouth, lips like the silk-spun
cocoon of the transforming moth, house of the warmed glossal,
anchored frenulum and eight muscles of the tongue;
lap and wash you with the milky galaxy of my spit.

You taste of copper-heavy pennies, a blacksmith's token,
which is to say you taste of the metallic tang of hemoglobin,
protein of plasma's scarlet cousin, the marrow of your bones,
a bone's broth. A roux of flour and fat, rising to the surface.
Together we make love to each other's
perfectly imperfect perfected bodies.

I tell you, I love licking your scars.

And as a mother would, I bathe you in my lapping,
forging conciliatory palate, moist-heavy
innate medicine of my mouth.

I want to bless you, anoint you in my saliva.
Holy water of the ceremonial fount, purification
of the sacrament. Uvula ululating and searching.

I tell you, I love licking your scars,
testament of the flesh,
petroglyphs of your death-
defying stories. You blazing with a mesmeric
proudful self-satisfaction, rapture
with the marring of your skin.

The adventuring bravado of your youthful joy, lack of fear
for death, that old and tiresome herringbone twill,
flax fibril of the shroud.

Along your forearm, the newest, boldest collection
of serrated scars etched haphazard, wild with new injury;
shiny and glistening woven epidermis. Frenetic skin stitched
by the making and remaking of you.

Cartography of the glossy, bone-white fiber.
A spider's spinneret, impressive
pulling your white blood cells back
together again.

You are the busy opaline peacock spider
of the Indus Valley, sapphire tarantula, iridescent
and galactic in color, a spindle
golden orb weaver

spinning, spinning, spinning
your web of connective tissue
back together again,
again back together,
you spin yourself.

Body always busy
with the labor of your healing,
when not belabored with its own destruction.
Always this reanimation of the keratin,

melanin monochromatic color wheel
of all shades brown.

I will find them one by one,
unearth each ameliorated laceration.
Linger over them with the papilla of my tongue,
pointed sharpened arrowhead
of my pursed and wetted lips.

Love and languish your blemishes,
the way you balk at pain, embrace
the breaking open of the skin,
place faith in the power of revivification.

I lick them one by one, your scars.

Your scars, spiral of nebulous interstellar clouds,
ionized Andromeda born of the Pillars of Creation,
light spectra of the supernova.

I tell you, I like licking your scars.

Almost as much as I like flaunting these words
I write, heliotrope of my powers, pulsing synonyms
for cicatrix, a scar on the bark of a tree.

Poems that bathe
your marred skin with my lovestruck
syntax of speechlore, which is to say
that I love you beyond words. Which is
to say that you are my forever foe, battle-weary
beau and black-out drunk fuck and phantasm.

I tell you, I love licking your scars.

Eating Slivers of Oranges With You In Your Bed

It must have been 7 am by the look of the light
slipping her silky rays through the blinds of your
bedroom window. Maybe 7:30 am, but it was definitely,
definitely Sunday.

The kind of Sunday perfumed with our *justpastdawn* love making,
sugared sweat, morning breath lazy with last night's tequila and salty
lime indulgences. The air scented by the tousling of our skin as we
turned and turned and writhed in your sheets, brown bodies toasting
the celebration of our young love and lust.

For we are young, even me which you made me believe,
that I am. Young. In love, maybe. Definitely, me.
Me, who is in love.

In love. But, it was definitely Sunday. You brought an orange to our bed,
and it was saccharin and juicy like a clementine but bigger, rounder, thicker
in the rind. You gnawed at its flesh with your savage and lovely white teeth
to open up its bouquet of fragrance. It made me think of Californian orchards
and long winding rows of trees alit with the blazing of god's best baubles.

Made me think of the words: *saffron, persimmon, fire, flame, coral, cinnabar.*

A gift. A present opened on Christmas day, but it was not Christmas, though
definitely, definitely Sunday. Maybe 7. Maybe 7:30 in the morning.

I kept my eyes closed, breasts bared, naked legs warmed beneath
your navy blue sheets. I felt smooth and soft and my body was at least
a mile long in length. I was a goddess rising, moving into a new day.
I was an open pearl, gushing, gathered with your oils between my legs.
I was blind and searching, seeking with my mouth.

And then you placed one fibrous sliver after the next onto my lips.
It was good and rich. It was pulpy and juice-filled connective tissue of
the white, webbed membranes. There were no seeds, rather pure sugar
of the vesicle. I was blind and thirsty and kept
my eyes closed as the body of the fruit slid down my throat.

I, a baby bird, and you
a doting mother. Feeding me.
Feeding me. I was *alive, alive, alive*
burning with gold, food of fortune.

I was only one of the five human senses:
Tang. Relish. Palate. Sapidity. Flavour.

I, who crested and catapulted as an oceanic wave does,
and the taste of it was.
And the taste of it. Was.

I thought of the Sanskrit word for orange: *nāraṅga.*
My mother tongue cried: *naranja.*
I thought of marmalade and of fingers on fire,
flames like little orange flickering cats' tongues.
I was a run-on sentence, a wild horse in a pasture of desire,
a woman opening into an ecstatic epiphany. Finally,
finally I was:

Laranja
Xopaltic
Orenge
Iwolintshi
Cempoalxochitl

It was Sunday and you, my beloved
Indio man,
brown man
made of river clay and red dirt,
brought an orange to our bed.

A fiery, orange like a little blaze
in the palm of your hand.
A small planet.

I have decided this is the way
you say *you love me.*

Last Night I Sat in the Grass

The perimeter of the streetlamp cast
bright around me like a large halo, icy white and
my shadow played against the green. I was
drunk, to be sure, stoned on my daughter's
coveted weed and the two dogs grazed like mild cows.
Cud-heavy and fattened with the night.
A sturdy half-moon shone in the sky, brighter

still than the human lights of that man-made city.
I was stoned, alone and so I swayed between bemusement,
comedy, wrath and the minute observations one
makes floating the way one does on Indica.

I wrote a poem in my head. Erased it. Wrote
another, erased that. I sounded like Plath, then
Hemingway then Olds, Santiago Baca, to be sure,
and finally like every other
brown poet writing about being brown sitting
in the vastness of green. A bug bit my knee,
my right forearm, the skin near my labia and the itch
was a stinging reminder that my body was mine.

I have nothing to say, and everything to feel.
I am blade and tussock. I am the slice of a bone-white
moon. My big dog vomited near the trunk of the
apricot tree. The little one snuffed about.
Uninterested, hairy, slinky.

Apricot is an Arabic word,
but first it was owned
by the Greek tongue, somewhere along the line
Latin, too. It is an early-ripening fruit.

I think I am too early. Or perhaps, I am too late.
I am stoned, and the grass smells like my
childhood opened at the kneecap, fruity
feverish, fertile, fleeting. Bloody with pulp.

Last night I tried to write a poem,
but it did not sound like me,

so I gave up, stared at the moon instead,
silver-stringed crescent, scythe-like and dangerous.
The dogs grazed like little cows, eating grass

to induce a good shit,

later.

I was stoned. I watched the moon.
The streetlamp. My shadow cast
against the green. They ate the grass,
unfettered, unbothered, unmoored
by words or nighttime or broken hearts.

Or cancer.
Or addiction.
Or the pressure and pleasure of writing a poem.

They just ate the grass,

those dogs, like fat-hooved and mild milk cows.

I was stoned.

Later

they will have the best shit
of their lives.

A Love Poem to Old Love Poems

I thought I had lost your ear, the liking
of my words from me to you. They fell
on deaf tympany, as an empty resonant sound
of the drummed abdomen does. My poems began
to lack the aplomb of your admiration, I think, or I
suppose I simply surmised and so I stopped writing
you your love poems. I stopped writing altogether
except for the purpose of money and obligation,
which is one in the same. ee cummings
said that love is more thicker than forget
but sometimes, I'm not sure, so instead
I doodle images of black and white koi
on perforated pages of notebook, illustrate
lopsided pencil-scratched pomegranates,
and once in awhile I sketch eyelids and eyeballs
and eyelashes and pupils imbedded in irises
and so it goes. I do all of these things instead
of writing poems for the sheer purpose to
not write poems of love to you, about you,
of you, despite you, inflamed by you. You
used to like my offerings, flimsy moth-netted
tokens of love, my largest sacrifice which
is how writers draw their own blood and
milk it at the feet of their beloved. Though no
more, for I thought I had, maybe this is
true, still do think that you have lost your interest.
I have lost your ear. I used to write about fiery
orange peels, citrus juice dribbling down our chins,
your bodily Lichtenberg scars etched petroglyphs
into the brown heat of your skin, Basc pears russet
cheeks, sin, transgression, joy, cum-soaked sheets,
the slope beneath your two eyes, polymath
of my desire, and all sorts of other lovely things.

All sorts of lovely things did I write.

I used to write of *lengua, sabor,* 8,000 taste buds
of umami, which in Japanese means essence
of deliciousness. I once wrote that you were the
13th moon of the longest year of my life. I used to
write all sorts of lovely things, for you.

Maybe this is the most beautiful procedure,
after all, you falling out of love with me falling
out of love with my love poems for you.
Still I will write it all down, now, the penultimate
poem of how one animal once loved another
animal and how two animals became
two people who fell out of love;

first one with the other,
and the other with the first.

If this were a different poem, I would write how
I will always remember that one particular
late autumnal afternoon we biked to the river.
The cranes were golden and the whole sky was
a sunset melting down around us as we kissed
with cold lips. The cranes were flaxen feathered
creatures and you still loved my poems. Then.
That was then, when I had your ear and you
still loved my love poems of you.

If this were a different poem I would write
that I remember how the water was a tapestry
of writhing ribbons, wet auriferous veins alive
with the cold, gold of that late afternoon. How
I remembered your clay colored lips upon mine
and I shivered with a resplendent fever, the sun
dripping down my neck and along the long spine
of my back, if this was that kind of poem.

But, this is not that poem
and I have lost your ear.

Instead, I will go and sketch a feather,
the face of an analog watch, grandfather clock
a little lone koi dancing across the paper.
And nary will I write a poem to fancy your ear.

The White Raven

after Pablo Neruda

I do not love you as the writer loves the pencil, graphite black
And salt of the sex, coal abrasion birthed of a pigmented, pregnant
Clay: instrument of the lying, fickle heart. The poet's best friend.

I am made more of secretive things, where the ravens go.
To be alone with one another. Along left behind dusted trails lined
By the oldest cottonwood trees, bent low, gnarled ancient things.

I love you as mycelium loves the fruiting body of the dark
Canals of rooting soil do spring forth the raw buds of dead leaves.
I am the glossy hollow-boned fingers of a common raven,
Beak-heavy with an impolite truth. My love does not lie for
You, rather, I am a many-hearted, honest verisimilitude
Of the wood-wind instrument.

Truth be, I love you like a conspiracy, flock of serendipitous, foraging clades.
Ink-wetted feathered blades, soft and sharp to the touch. I am the
Impenetrable cloak and you the twelve seeking arrows.

I do not love you as the fable loves the dogmatic moral, rather
I love you simply, open eyed as the fluted pipe, a spine, a stairwell,
A ladder placed against the walls of your heart and all the earth is flame.

I love you like a book with no name, the song of songs scorched
By Apollo's torch. O' immaculate chamber of this heart tethered
To your heart and I hope you will not leave me. Let me always

Embrace your human form, and may my lungs breathe your
Breath and hold it still within the ticking clock's arms, half-
Past midnight and beyond the trembling witching hour.

I am neither your religion nor your sinning.
I am your dripping topaz, salt-rose salvation.

I will give you my ear. My mind. My solace.
My attention. My centrifugal listening soul.
I will quiet the trembling fleeing, fleeting foal of my
Twitching brain. I will calm myself and listen for your name.
I will make still my machinations and the center will hold.
I will make my body your nesting home, twine and blade of grass.

The moon is my redemption, your bed of hair my altar, the
Streets palmed within your hands, my blushing supplication.
I will bring myself back to earth for you, and leave behind my brutish fear.

I need not to possess you, but love and cherish you, creamy-
Sweetened melody-making man. I only want to sleep next to you,
Harmonized oceans of shivering dreams, vibrating lute
Strings of the shared lungs pulling synchronized deep,

Deep, watercolor paintings of the enlivened minds.
I want to be your artist and you mine. Twilight bounds
Drunk in the peaceful watchtower of a moon-brightened
Emptying night. Serpent of light. Blood orange dawn, bright.

And when we wake, side by side, your body as fresh as a plum,
Oh, how bright our bright is shared fleshly single bed is,
Warmed by the scent of our sleeping torsos syncopated thrum.

My heart is a drum.
My heart is a drum.

Bright is the light that my poem
Carves the way. Oh, how I hope you stay.

The second life of the white raven,
Birthed of black,
Impossibly bright.

How I hope for you, for me,
For us, that you will always stay.
How I hope we become the light.

How I hope we become the
Unconditional, everlasting love

Of our light.

I Wrote You a Love Song On the Back of a Bible

after Drive-By Truckers

It was blood drunk and the words were welt with salt and indigo ink
and I ain't no religious lady, but I love me some saints and martyrs,
the way they die by fire, crucifix rust of the nail, tears and lament, wails
of a funeral pyre. A good country song makes me see God,

smell his wrath and revenge and woesome loneliness deep
in the cavern of my darkened *smokechoked* nicotine nostrils.

drives me to drink
the stink of whiskey, to purr
against some stranger's body
somewhere of some damnable, foolish dance floor
in the middle of nowhere town,
smelling of wood chips and pine shavings, fall
down from the pedestal
of my favorite pair of stilettos, spilling
into the street and out of a neon-lit bar,
where the poets and pirates swill the glass-bottom
suds of love songs, unrequited guilt down their gullets,
ash their *cigarillos* onto the floor, fight
and flail and then land cow-fatted on their asses,
a clown splatter across
the wetted pavement.

On a good night, I remember my bible,
dog-earred, tucked away
in my bedside table, onion-veined,
paper-thin sheets of dogma stamped
in Gutenberg typeface font. The one grandma
gave me when she used to believe
my soul could be saved. She don't think that
no more. On good nights, I rip the binding of that
good book. Etch rambling words and lyrics into
and onto and into it. These are my prayers, these
days. They say, I loved once, or maybe it was

just fascination and fanaticism having some fun
late last night, eeking into the watery, weary hours
of a morning blur.

Maybe it was the television blaring evangelist
hellfire to the rhythm of my dreams as I fell, fell,
fell to sleep,

writing you a love song, a love song
on the back of a bible.

And some good ol' boy sang to my pain.
And some good ol' boy sang to my pain.

The Proof Will Be My Body

After Louise Glück

The proof will be hot fingered prints oiled across the glass,
sheets like soiled feathers, thick liquid spilled atop my belly,
as you, a dagger steaming point your aimed body, bull's eye
deep into the center of me and I cry out like a flock of birds,
scattered by the cracking-opened sound of a bullet exploding
a gray winter sky. This is how you pry open my
melancholy, peer into the bleeding garnet of the menses.

I am a smattering of crows shattering the milkweed of the day,
sudden flapping black wings, shiny with a blue onyx,
glittering black crown of the bare-faced carrion.
I will prove to you time and time again, no matter how
and in whatever ways you ask, cajole, demand of me –
that which is my worship of you. I will gift you my
bejeweled and beloved secret middle name. For you, the proof
will be my body, flushed with fire
lit by your heavy, heavenly hefty flinty hands.
My skin imprinted with your fevered pulse.
I am the petal of the tongue, pollen and poison.
I am ashamed with how much love
I carry for you. I am the stalking puma,
Pablo's savage harvest.

Forgive me, love. I did not mean
to turn you into a meal, but you
are the sleek meat I hunger for.
You are the proof that the body
responds and betrays itself.

It always responds,
Judas of the truth.

We Are Not Birds

> *Each day I think of you I fumble an attempt to fly to impress you*
> *with the color of my paper wings.*
> —*Felonies and Arias of the Heart, Frank Lima.*

We are not birds, but today I saw a bulky, brown hawk perch
on a wire fence not far from my home. I made sure to put the
chihuahua inside, for hawks are known to pluck them from their
yards, spindly miniature appendages flapping and mouths yawping,
while they take them somewhere to eat them alive. I couldn't fathom
my dear little dog, eyes pecked to death in some feathery dungeon
of that bird. Bowels loosened from the sac of soft stomach and swallowed
clean, masticated by the mama and regurgitated into and inside the gullets
of a squawking downy, insatiable bevy of baby birds. I don't want for her
to be eaten alive.

I am not a bird, but I preen for you.
I clean my feathers but no one
sees, especially not *you*.

If I were a bird,
I would peer at you
unnoticed from a light pole
outside of your window. Wait
for you to leave your home,
for you to stretch in the morning sun,
brown muscles
of the chest and torso rippling,
blue jeans and no shoes.

This is what I would do,
if I was a bird.

There is no beauty like yours. A bejeweled bull's
eye for my birdish, murderous aim.
I would swoop, aiming for your guts, your heart,
your left eyeball and take what I could. I would

devour that which I could hold in my little bird belly,
beak bloodied with your lifeforce and gelatinous
soupy alloy of the eye. I am in love with the
gore like that, sensual sex of survival of the
fittest, axe of the apple. Lift you
haphazard into the sky,
no matter if you were
too heavy to hold. I would try.

Clasp with orange and purple-blue veiny claws,
hooked talon of the calcium into your neck.

As if in a dream, I would be a predator and you my prey.
My little pet, rodent, smaller petty bird. My bitch in heat.
My paper wings would sing like a chartreuse-hued diaphanous
Chinese kite whistling with wind. I would impress
you with my attempt to kill you, finally. You will notice me.
My delicate rage and paper wings. If I was a bird, and gladly
I am not.

I fumble at letting
you go.

The Heart is a Hundred Mouths Open

After Dorianne Laux

It is still siphoning the energy from where I gave you a hand
job in front of the corner-street Catholic church just down the road
from my quaint home. How we rode the swings, laughed in the
face of God, watched the night roil black and spit out stars.
Oily hot skillet spittle sky. It was summer. We played in the corner-
neighborhood grass-juice of the public park.

We sizzled with sin and two bodies became one.

I should have known then that you were a passing train,
wrecking the night with your sound. Pollution taint with noise,
roaring louder than my brain could catch up with. We salivated.
Simpered. Sauntered. Postured. Leapt into the fire, two liars.

We opened our mouths a hundred times wide, and you made
jovial of it all. The plaster saints looked on and religion was
a passing thought. The heart is a hundred mouths open, thousands
of swords in my shank, a cross and albatross to bear. *Una prieta.*
Entry point of the fleshly wounds punctured by the long-handled spears.

I am still gaping, hungry.
Never to be satiated.
A room full of doors.

We are 10,000 wagging, red and hot tongues flickering
like a mighty forest aflame.
We are 10,000 wagging, red tongues waving into the air.
Scarlet-fingered and fucked sideways.

I knew what I signed up for. But, still I have my regrets.
I am a worshiper without a fount, roving without a throne.

A hundred mouths gaping, blood-tongued Kali,
lapping up the blackness.

A pair of hands without a home.

Pink Bed

You rolled like a sandwich wrap in my pink sheets, pink
blanket, pink linen-encased pillows swathing your black-corkscrew
haired head in my full-bodied, florid bed. Your black mustache and your black
beard and your black sideburns, burning onyx against my blushing, rose
petal pink, pink-on-pink bed. My sanguine, blooming cheap cotton sheets,
frill of the ruffle-dust-skirt, pink for the sake of pink. Your man cheeks, rubicond
flushed ruddy red and glowing, *labios* like a pair of naked mollusks making love.
Lips for me to bite, bleed, burn with my teeth. Suture of the pink. Pure and pink
like the dawn rising in the East over the cusp of the Sandias. Watermelon
pink. Carnation pink. Rosa de Virgen de Guadalupe Church on Sunday pink.
Pink like my clit. Pink lick, slit of wrist. You freckled skin, a hue that is the cousin of
pink, tickling pink, sipping on the nectar of an armpit pink. Pink ink of a ballpoint pen.
Upside down, inverted soul of the pinkish pinky tickling the taint, piano keys pink.
Drum roll pink. Guitar string slice of pink, thinking of the flesh of the peach, apricot,
pink of nectarine pink.

You are pink like that. When you come over. Visit me, with an explosion of spontaneity
drunk with the hybrid fusion of pink, I am the inside of the inside of the color of pink.

For what is pink? Cherry blossom pink. Dianthus pink.
Pink flamingos in flight over Pocharam Lake in Andhra Pradesh,
India. Pink, I think.

Your hair is so black. So long and void of all color, which is to say that is all of the colors.
Prism kaelidoscopic pink, therefore the lack of pink. Your hair is so black. Your
eyes painted by the root of the sassafras, root beer bark. Your multitude of
bodied freckles, a watercolor singing a song of Impressionism. You are not pink,
until you beckon to me. Lay in my bed of pink pillows, pink cotton, satin, velvet, a
gala of languid, lounging pink. And you sleep.

You sleep in my pink bed. You breathe and writhe and cum in my bed. Atop me.
Inside of me. Beside me. Behind me. You are the pink wash of the sun streaming
through my morning window.

Together we become the rosy birth of a petal bud. Blooming.

Pink for the sake of pink. For the sake of love.

You rolled like a sandwich wrap
in my pink bed.
Lovely. Soft.

Warm with love.

In the Morning He Cries Pink Thinking of
His Grandfather

Left eye leaks a *thinthick* trail of water.
It hovers a bit in the corner pocket of his lashed eye.
Spills over and catches the slight kiss of his crow's feet.
Slides down the skin of his cheek, stippled by a bouquet
of ecru freckles, tawny as raw silk.

It is the most translucent, fragile rivulet I have ever seen.
A bit, it hesitates, gathering a pool of thought, dulcet liquid,
little diamond of the heart.

He heaves slightly and the lip quivers, chest pulsates with light.
His full-bodied lungs and breath. His beautiful head rests
upon my pillow. Body a metronome for his memories and sweet sorrow.
He is a chamber orchestra and the fifty musicians within him create a song.

It is the morning and the sun is early, tipping over the mountain.
Ready to break open the sky with a soft gauzy hue, but
the eastern horizon lets us have this moment, a paused
pendulum, for just a bit, a bit of this moment, the two of us.

My bedroom is the *inbetween* time.
In between sleep and wake.
In between night and dawn.
In between sunrise and blazing morning.
In between life and death and love and loss and loss is love and so on.

My bedroom window is a vigilant saint,
and quells the new light of the day.

It is Carravagio's Assisi in ecstasy, demure glaze
of the walnut oil, a lightly painted chiaroscuro tableau.

One dog sleeps beneath the bed, the other outside
howling at the yellow school bus kids, who are

prematurely early and grumpy and trudging
their feet across new and unexpected lives.

But we are nude beneath my sheets and the hair
of his left thigh is a cross-hatch of soft dark moss.
It tickles the inside of my eager knee and my ankle
is wrapped around his firm muscled calf and this
is how we share the almost-just-upon-us morning.

He speaks of his grandfather and how he lived
in a house on a cliff, how his *abuelo* never fired his gun,
whittled a wooden book instead,
and placed the metal of it
inside for safekeeping.

He speaks of his grandfather's soft lessons and how he misses
that kind man. Oh, how he misses that kind man who fathered him
and then the second and third trail of salted water falls, quick from
his angled eye and onto my pink pillow. I see a droplet sit there a bit
and then absorb into the silent threads, the way soil takes to the rain
feeding the foliage. I place one brown hand upon the center of his wide
chest. It is a drumbeat alive with sound.

He shudders, the way a season might shift and shudder into the next
season and the next. Slow but with the need to transform, recede and
emerge again. The way water falls from the heavens and births that which
was once dead, but also still alive. And we are pleased with this surprise.

This is how we love.
This is how he cries.

It makes me think of the best lines of poetry I have ever suffered,
the most sumptuous work of art I have ever witnessed: a renaissance
made into man, man of letters made into story and how a poem
is created by the brushstroke dipped in memories:

> *Drink to me only with thine eyes,*
> *And I will pledge with mine;*
> *Or leave a kiss but in the cup,*
> *And I'll not look for wine.*

When his eyes shine with tears,
amber as an agave honey,
I have found that I will lap them
with my tongue.

Place my lips upon the jeweled topaz
of his waters and suckle him.

He is the kindest man I know.

And his sorrow is mine
and I will hold him
until the salt
becomes solid
and dissolves
back into the earth.

A crystal gem born of the body
of his remembering. His recollection
of his grandfather's everlasting spirit.

A man who loved him when he was a boy.
A man who loves him still across time,
across the veil of life and death and life.

Sus antepasado.

The eternal cempasúchil.
Twenty petals of the flower
of the heart.

In the morning he cries pink,
thinking of Miguel, his grandfather,
Miguel, that lovely man whom he
loved and who loved him.
And for that,
I will always
taste his grief.

His tears upon

my tongue,
my lips,
willingly,
my beloved.

I will hold it
there,
his grief,
inside of me,
because I love
him more than
he may know.

His grief,

a wet solid pearl,
soft tissue of his tear.

I will hold it
until he
needs
it back.

Calls
it home
once
more.

I Will Feed You Golden Pride BBQ Chicken
Because I Love You

I will tuck you into my pink linen-clad, sheeted bed, lay your head
Upon my lilac *flores*-printed pillows and feed you BBQ chicken
For the rest of your days, because I love you. I will unravel your
Curls from atop your head, the corkscrew craziness that holds
Together your patchwork of music-making thoughts and feed you
Snacks. If this is what it takes to hold you, keep you in the glass-
Bottomed pendulum of my heart, inside the inside of me where
My love forms like foam and fog-thickened devotion. I will buy
You all of the chicken from that *Burque* chicken shack, *Boricua* boy,
Island boy, boy not afraid to walk barefoot upon my desert-riddled, sand-
Dusted-tiled floor, 1950s neighborhood throwback house, tucked into
The corner pocket of North East Heights snobbery and the glamor of
The vagabond homelessness of our unsheltered relatives, sticking needles
Into their arms. Here I live within this faded track-housing glory
boasting decades-old economy, rich ballast and braggadocious, ball-busting
bloated, outdated gentrification.

Because I love you and you are not afraid of me,
I'll feed you blue-corn chips,
Frontier-toasted BLTs,
Red chile without too much heat, and lip you with a golden honey
Woven of my mouth and silky-spindled, glossened hot-spittle kisses.

I'll rub your tummy, with all of that blackened swirled, smoothed
Rounded downy hair, and wish you a goodnight prayer,
poem, blessing scented with the burning sticks of Palo Santo lit
by the small fires made between my legs and fingers and fingers and legs.
I will make of you an *Ofrenda*, effigy, Zozobra burning bright upon the
black summer-salted night. I will make every day our first kiss,
first fuck, first date, first love.

I won't take you for a *pinche* ride on that *pinche* Art Bus, instead
I will gather your limbs and place you into the corn pollen pouch

latched around my neck. From there, I will take you to all of the places
we have ever dreamed of.

Tijeras trails mucking the dirt, *Managua, Nicaragua, Costa Rica,*
Our first Carlos Sanatana concert, Tunnel Canyon, the golden banks
of *La Jefita Rio Grande.*

Lit by a dusk-colored Autumnal light. The slow burning, melting sun
Waving goodbye as it sinks low between the horizon of cottonwood delight.

I will feed you Golden Pride BBQ Chicken while you lounge forever in
My bed, two dogs snoring between our legs, the lazy oscillating fan humming
Our favorite good morning and good night tunes. You are the October Aries
moon and I, your white-haired, belly-fatted Capricorn goat. I shall call you
By my name and you will forget the ways I quickly age. Together we are

The newness of a *Mexica* bloodletting, sacrificial day. *Todos dia de los
Muertos nacido del colibrí iridiscente.* We will grow old and fattened,
Juiced by the meat of the bone. *Creo en tu carne. Los pájaros conocen
todos los idiomas.*

Even if they die for love.
Even if they eat or are
eaten by the heart of the human.

Human humming.
Humming the heat
And meat of love.

God Left Me to Wonder

And so I said, God, you are a stubborn father.
And so I said, God you are a neglectful mother.
And so I said, God you are a disappointing lover.
And so I said, God, give me two hands and they did.
And so I held my child, a slippery wet seal slid
from the slalom of my body into the dust of this earth.
And it was good.

And so I said, God; *bounty, booming,*
become, birth.

And so I heard nothing. God is and was
radio silent. Radium. God is science and magic.
White noise and static. The sound of a polygon,
electric fences and a feathery snow dusting
the dark-horned Adirondacks.

Which is to say, God, oh God,
is luxuriously mute. God is not an
algorithm or phosphorescent line of laptop
glowing green binary code.

God is too clever for that.
God is meat, lust, sweat and pulp.

And so I said, God, I hate you.
And so said God, I don't care.
God, I said, I wonder about you sometimes.
And so said God, you contemplate
that which is you.
And God said,
God is God.

God, you are honest and wicked. Wicked
with glee. I am God, I say to God.

God said, yes.

God gave me two hands. Hands, that I
gave myself. For I am divine. God in the
flesh. The in-between Nephalem.

Grasping at God. Goading
God. Invoking God. Weeping
at the altar of God's feet. I went

to war

with God and won. God
succumbed.
For, I am triumphant
like Gabriel's blazing
brass horns, blaring,
bleating, bellowing.

God is the garden of joy and sex,
sorrow and death.

I believe. God is apocrypha.

I suffer. I churn. My brain has been on fire for
forty-three long years.
I am strange and wondrous and wise with weary.
God is neither good nor bad.

I ponder. God is funny like that.

And so I said, God, *look*.

My hands.
My hands.

My alive and pulsing hands!

Still, for Billie

with a gardenia or two in her hair
tucked behind that silken ear tuned
as a silver string taut and wound
by an old clear voiced lute neck
deep round cavity of a harmonious
ochre body

it is here that I suspend beneath
her music this fine and mellow Sunday
bound by a Lester Young tune grainy black
and white whimsy and it is Sunday and I feel
melancholy and it is Sunday and I scrape potato
peels into the kitchen sink
and it is Sunday

I am readying dinner dirt drunk scent of the earth
and the starchy good root cares not
if it is alive or dead then I witness
a watery sunset through the porthole
of my sunken window as the sun lowers
its body into my winter garden a ball of yellow
and my house points west
small sacred cardinal compass

she of all *shes*
Billie rustic and regal queen
croons long dead though so alive
and warm buttery songstress voice
filling my small oven *heavywomb* warmed home,
a golden lasso sprung forth from
that godly radio

a murmuring glimmering glow worm
she of all *shes* croons

a flame lit torch song and it is Sunday
sunset-flaxen Sunday
pink rose and smokey quartz sky of a Sunday,
the in-between
blue gloom of the gloam-soaked Sunday

Last of the loooooong arm of winter,
full Snow Moon Sunday
and I am peeling russet potatoes
into the porcelain mouth of sink
maybe I'll cook them in grease
hot spittle of skillet
fat of the dead

I remember, tangential as it seems
that gardenias do bloom, if not now,
if not this season sometime somewhere
and soon, soon white flowery snow-drenched
petals supple as a young woman's cheek

My man he don't love me
Treats me oh so mean
He's the lowest man
That I've ever seen
But when he starts into love me
He is so fine and mellow

it is Sunday and I know
love turns off and on
like a faucet
it turns off and on and off and I,

I am a foolhardy desirous acolyte
of all things painful and noble
all things that grow live and take
their time to die
luxurious lazy notes that slide
down the throat

bitch of the elixir
hounds of hell
baying at a hot moon

and on this Sunday
still I love her
this apocryphal Judas kiss of a Sunday

still, still
I love her,
still

Tonight, in Albuquerque

I did not come here to utter truth,
usually I honey-lie and sing my own praises,

a warbling Bukowski bluebird pining
for the familiar nest of trauma, you don't

listen or listen for my flaws anymore, and I miss them,
those cocky inconsistencies, ballistic of the bullet

gunpowder beauties, birthed by regret and trigger
unhappy itching flickering fingers. Crosshairs, lines

and right angles of my thighs, optical eyepiece
sniper of the high-precision pussy, predator snapping
at prey.

I, who snap at prey, with an iron jaw.

Tonight we are two brown bodies forgetting. Fraught
we are, with grins like bows and sliced open eyes slivered by arrows,

tactical in scope, we muddy your blue sheets with an ivory
soaked body blush made of our combined cum, seminal seminary
of Vitamin C and an acidic excited protein, lube, loss, lovelorn.

This, I think, is better than the color red.

Tonight we are two brown bodies sliding with sweat,
a snail's solid and sticky gel, flooded mucous of the membrane.

We wrestle, arms and legs locked ancient in a grappling that is
more about violence and less about love, though we say freely,

the word, *love.*

Pretending to look but looking into the nothing of
each other's eyes. We are out of range. Tonight
in Albuquerque, you

are the bird and I am the gun. Or I am the gun and you
the bird. Neither of us are falling in or out of love.

Who is the spearhead? Who is the poison?
Who is the victor? Who is the spoiler?

When did I become so wretched with the need to plunder?
Who are you fucking? Me or her or you or what?

My Latest Dream and You Did Not Die

though, when you do and I awake,
I *hardhug* you for thirty seconds while you twitch
a feral cat lit on fire from all four paws up
and I am happy that you are alive.

You don't hug the way you did when you were two.
I was twenty three when I expelled you,
parturition bags of gooey fluid burst forth,
amniotic flood betwixt moon-heavy thighs,
or so the doctor said.

I didn't want you, and that is the damned truth.
You'll read this poem one day and condemn me to hell,
but that is what we call a mother's love.
How we lie, ephemeral contradictions that hide
complicated genomes of gestation and blue-printed maternity.

But when I *overworry*, like I do from time to time,
I dream that you have crashed your car into an aluminum
accordion, T-bone
of metal amalgamation on the corner
of Odelia and Edith Avenue,
and I place tulips at your grey, grey gravestone.
You are a closed casket in my dream.
I, a mother, weeping with fire.

Or I dream that a gang of hooligan frat boys have,
in their fanatic rape-fantasy frenzy,
lured you to the woods, and you
a doll-faced damsel in distress
are dismembered and strewn among the mulch.
Gerber Daisies sprout from your half-buried limbs,
oxeye of aster, spoon-shaped petalled disks.
Or I dream that your white blood cells

are leukemia-marred, multiplicitous
bone marrow heated by a cancerous magma,
and I hold close your withered body of youth
while you dissolve into the bedsheets.

I dream like this sometimes. Horrid,
bewildered machinations of a mother
who loves and loves
her daughter.

Grisly, I know, but the mice in my brain
go on and on in their woeful laments.
Macabre, mysterious, morose.

I had one too many abortions to mention
per politeful conversation, all
before I carried you full term.
And this is the damned truth.

Then you happened. A swimming silver
fish in utero, suspension of the pear-shaped
placenta. I was balloon-bellied and smitten with oranges
and chocolate ding-dongs,
eating my way through nine-months,
betrothed to a man who didn't love me.

Your father did not love me.
And I thought, used to think, that I did not
want you. How foolish and lame-hearted
and I hope to know that other mothers
who love their daughters as fiercely
as I love you thought those same thoughts too.

Now, I hug your nineteen year old *wellearned* body and you
do not want to hug me back. You want to carouse,
go to trap music concerts in the desert,
wear no-show socks and lace-up thongs,
buy feathery long, long fake eyelashes

and paste them to your face. You ask me
for money and eat burritos at 1 am
while watching Jersey Shore, ad infinitum.

You paint butterflies and dead girls upon bone-white canvas,
until the bulb burns thin and the dogs begin to howl.

You want five dollar soy chai lattes and a brand new car.
You want skater shoes and sweet potato fries.
You want college and therapy and creamy expensive face washes.

I don't mind. I'll give it all to you.
I'll give you the world. Lawn tickets,
school supplies, unsolicited advice,
30 second hugs, blood-red roses whittled of wood,
purple-ink pens, graph paper, potted succulents
that you leave to die
on your windowsill.

Not because guilt, guilt, guilt.
Because of love, love, love.

Sometimes I dream of your death, wake
sobbing and then check
in on your sleeping, breathing body
at rest in the neighboring room.

Knowing you are alive,
knowing I almost didn't
let you live.

I Fell In Love With Bukowski Again

Because he is a crude and raffish piece of shit,
And that is my favorite kind of poem to light fire to.

Because he is unbridled, once-upon-a-time wild horse
Made to beg like a pauper for nothing no how

Because he is big-nosed and pock-marked like my father,
Ragged as my dead grandfather, my father's whiskey soaked father

Because he is a polack beat by the belt of his angered red father
Swinging from the shower curtain rod of some Los Angeles bathroom apartment

Because he knows a good violent story when he hears one, and tells of it
Because he is a red-hot blooded man and so am I

Because like him I like to test my friends with wonders of mom-suicide
And too-close dads and memories of children tossed into the wilderness of the
street

The night slathering with a wild dripping open wolf mouth eating them whole

They pretend they like my stories, my friends they pretend they like
my kind of poems, my friends

I pretend to be aghast at that which is Bukowski,
but reading him is like coming home

Reading him is like losing my second skin,
like fucking a stranger until I black out

My Ex-Husband Whose Father Died

And I should have sent flowers, marigolds to light his way.
And I should have written a poem then, but I am writing it now.
And I should have told my Ex-Husband's sisters that Khalil Gibran said of death,

For what is it to die but to stand naked in the wind and to melt into the sun?

And I should have cried a river made of salt for him, my Ex-Husband's
dead father, but wait, I did.
And I should have told my Ex-Husband's mother, let me hold your hand.
And I should have penned a letter to my Ex-Husband's father's grandchildren,
writ in ocean blue ink. And it could have sounded like the spray of foam.
And I should have drove to that small town of my Ex-Husband's father's
origin and left copal, palo santo ashes and lavender stalks at his grave.

And I should know where his father
is buried, but I do not.

And I should have opened my voice into the sound of, *Ohm* for my Ex-Husband's
father who is no longer alive. I should have ululated like the pure ring of a singing bowl.

And I should have called my Ex-Husband's father while he was still breathing,
when he lost his leg. I should have done that.

And I should have said, Glenn, you were a kind and quiet man and your home
was a warm alcove for my little daughter and I.

And I should have said, thank you and I love you.
And I should have said, Glenn, I remember how you toiled in the front yard of
your small town home, beneath the yawning mouths of the hoods of your rustic
cars. How you made art out of metal and piecemealed tiles. How you wore your
fedoras, tidy and proud upon your head.

And I should have said how much I admired your quietude.
How you only spoke when it meant something.
How your humor was sly and dry and wicked fun.

And I should have said,

Your life was like a ribbon, unfurling satin, soft and pale like a primrose.
Behind you and in front of you, your life went on unraveling and traveling again.
The sun rises in the East and sinks its slow, weary head in the West,
at peace for all perpetuity, and somewhere there is a cave that keeps the sound of your
voice in the belly of its dry, silt-lined sediment of the eternal spirited body. For matter can
neither be created nor destroyed. One day your children will arrive there, and their children
and their children too. They will sing your song and it will sound like the wind.

And I should have said to my Ex-Husband, I loved you because your father
raised you right.
And I should have said, Thank you for that, Glenn. Thank you for making a
man I loved deeply when we were in love, while we loved.
And I should have said, I was your daughter too.
For at least a small time. A small time.

Those were the good years.

I Listen to Bikini Kill and Launder My Underwear
While Drinking Light Beer

for Amanda Sutton, my favorite book lady

And my closet is an echo chamber, as I stuff last season's shoes into boxes,
Fold tidy thongs into little red and leopard print balls of fabric, marvel at how
Responsible I have become since this afternoon, since last night when I kissed,
Open mouthed, a stranger in front of the corner bar on Central Avenue and Gold.

I scream along to the discordant chords, but I won't use the word banshee.
I won't include the word, Feminist in this poem. I am the Queen of the Neighborhood,
And it's the fourth day of my period. When I bleed like this I tend to be loud,
Sloppy but also full of hope. I am the medicine. I smell of copper between the thighs,
Sweet grass and oil of the wild violet, self-seeding frenzy. I have left my angry boyfriend
for the fifteenth time,

If anyone is counting.

But no one is, least of all me. I bask in this glory and light
Mi Virgen de Guadalupe Tonantzin candle hoping this will be the last time.
Meaning, I am *leaving leaving leaving* him behind and listening to Bikini Kill.
I am punk as funk. I am the cycle breaker, the breaker of cycles.

My beer is tepid but I do not mind. My closet, an echo chamber as I scratch
open my throat, and I try on all of my own clothes.

Bikini Kill is a ragged bleeding itch and it is exactly what I needed. Bleating,
Large and dirty from my ten dollar portable speaker. I am drunk on shitty light
beer, high on half of a week-old joint, And this, this makes me beyond happy.

Single. Spinster. Salivating like a bitch in heat.

Vibe: A Poem of Resistance

in some places around the world
dance is a death sentence
A sharpened makeshift guillotine
for the electric twist and turn of
neck, the pulley of the *twistvibe*
of tendon, arched foot and calf—
poised wrist and flick of hand.
the freedom of the soul
and flight of dancer
wingspan, hipshake, piece de resistance
to dance is to be a revolution
name me rebel
name me bombshelter, rubble
dancing in the aftermath
border dweller poetess
name me the diviner of movement
freeflow
To VIBE with the forces of nature
that undulate around us is to pull
poesía y palabras from thin air—
to take the water, the molecule,
the oxygen and breath of the lung
to spin in fire
to make rain from movement
to pound the earth with bare foot,
mocassin and deer hide—
strike a flamenco heel
like a matchstick
the quick screech and scratch
of sneaker
BGIRL/BBOY fresh
to VIBE is to be a revolution
a mighty force of limb, lung and heart
in some places in the world
dance is a celebration

a testament to the freedom
of the soul
furious fight for flight
an everlasting love
for life
a dancer's trembling
breath

The Rain

Praise the rain
we make
together.

The way it wets and makes wetter
and even wetter still,
the threads of your midnight
cobalt bedsheets.

The way in which
your body, connected
to my body creates water
from the thin,
slim dry desert air.
How the writhing
pulls and pushes and pulls
a bounty of the juice.

Wrings us dry.

How the raininess
becomes a madness.

How the madness
becomes the prize.

How a raindrop takes
on the shape of a star-seed,
shed fruit of the duct.

It is the wine-apple grenade
of the teary-eyed pomegranate.
It is the rain loosened by the weary

shame-soaked mother.
The *deathdeathdeath*
of the father.

You Let Me Gather Clouds

Gather thoughts, stare out the moving
window of your transcendental, journeying
truck, white paint job like a pearl or a baby's first
tooth, fat tire of tread black on black rubber, rim
asphalt. Sometimes we chatter on and on,
as the miles glide by beneath us
10,678 elevated feet up the terrain we climb
to the peak of a crested view

Like old friends who knew each other, we vibe
as if from a past life, two chums sipping honey
sweetened country iced tea, on a slow Sunday
morning upon some crooked white-picket porch or
like we are fishing buddies seeking the silver
iridescent pink-tinged scales of the behemoth
salmon, knee-deep in fresh-water lakes opening up
into the torrential currents of an ice cold river.

Our conversations are a deluge, like that.
Scattered note drops creating a symphonic
jazz syncopation and we go on and on like that.

Other times we are silent and you let me
gather clouds in my head, my daydreams,
no pressure and I gaze at the sky without
the hotboil of expectation to entertain,
amuse, worship you at your altar. You don't
need me to say

anything. And I don't say anything. Instead,
I am busy thrumming with the aliveness of
my own musings, gathering clouds in my head,

plucking them from the spectral skies, putting
them into the basket of my mind like fattened
fluffs of cotton.

You are the fresh breeze that fills my lungs.

But when we do talk, utter conjectures, rambling
words wild like roses heavy with bloom,
thorn and thick stalk, it is about music and mountains,
dogma and island songs, Mexican ballads,
west coast oceans, passing thoughts about
our fathers, steel string guitar riffs and whatnot.

Everything is easy. Which is to say, this is love.
The clouds in my head are drifting things of the
human life and you like the way I human.

You love me more, even, for my fleeting patchwork
tangential, tangled meandering thoughts that I think,
oftentimes give voice to, even when I don't make
sensical meaning of it all. You know this is the way
I gather clouds in my head, let the rain wash down
from the top to bottom, pool and eddy at my feet, only
to be repeated in the neverending circular cycle of
evaporation, condensation, precipitation.

Cirrus. Cumulous. Nimbus. Stratus.

You like my rambling and my silences and I gather
clouds in my head. I thrum with a type of peace
and here I find my respite with you,
beside you,
because of
you.

Together we are secret things both separate from one another,
And paired at the same time. Air and land. *Tierra y Cielo.*
Ephemeral dewpoint of the atmospheric vapor, toiling in tandem.

You let me. And I let you.
I let you and you let me.

Which is to say we gather clouds,
billowy sails of the argonauts' voyage
across sea and sky.

Together we are luminance.
Apart we are the *clima* of the
orchestral stratosphere.

You let the sky touch
my face.

And then with my reaching hands,
I touch yours.

This is love.

About the Author

Jessica Helen Lopez is the City of Albuquerque Poet Laureate, Emeritus (2014-2016), a NM Humanities Chautauqua Scholar, Rural Women's Collective Fellow at Justice for Migrant Women and the Zia Book Award Recipient for her inaugural poetry collection, *Always Messing With them Boys (West End Press)*. She is also the author of *The Blood Poems (University of New Mexico Press)*, *The Language of Bleeding, Provocateur and cunt. bomb.(Swimming With Elephants Publications)*. An Adjunct Instructor with the University of New Mexico Chicana and Chicano Studies Department, Lopez also teaches at the Native American Community Academy High School, and the Santa Fe Institute of American Indian Academy. A California born Chicana, Lopez resides in Albuquerque, New Mexico. A six-time member of the ABQ Champion Winning Slam Team and two-time champion of the ABQ Women of the World Poetry Slam, Lopez is a member of the Macondo Foundation, an association of socially-engaged writers working to advance creativity, foster generosity, and serve community which was founded in 1995 by Mexican-American writer Sandra Cisneros. Lopez was the John Trudell Featured Activist Poet awarded by the San Bernardino College and is the editor of the photo-poetic anthology, *La Palabra: The Word is a Woman and Earthships: A New Mecca Poetry Collection*. Her poetry, academic research and book reviews have been published widely both in print and online. She is a single mama, Xingona, Jota, Pocha, and lover of lime paletas and fierce little chihuahuas. Visit her at **jessicahelenlopezpoet.wordpress.com**. Contact her at jessicahelenlopez@gmail.com.

FLOWERSONG
PRESS

**FlowerSong Press nurtures essential verse
from, about, and throughout the borderlands.
Literary. Lyrical. Boundless.**

Sign up for announcements about
new and upcoming titles at:

www.flowersongpress.com

www.ingramcontent.com/pod-product-compliance
Lightning Source LLC
Chambersburg PA
CBHW031446120626
46545CB00006B/2579